GREAT MINDS
of Ancient Science and Math

THE FATHER OF ANATOMY

GALEN AND HIS DISSECTIONS

Lisa Yount

Enslow Publishers, Inc.
40 Industrial Road
Box 398
Berkeley Heights, NJ 07922
USA

http://www.enslow.com

To John Scarborough
for giving research help "beyond the call of duty."

Library of Congress Cataloging-in-Publication Data

Yount, Lisa.
 The father of anatomy : Galen and his dissections / Lisa Yount.
  p. cm. — (Great minds of ancient science and math)
 Includes bibliographical references and index.
 Summary: "A biography of ancient Greek physician Galen, whose dissections of animals led to
discoveries about human anatomy. He was the authority on medical knowledge in the Western
world for more than fifteen hundred years"—Provided by publisher.
 ISBN-13: 978-0-7660-3380-1
 ISBN-10: 0-7660-3380-5
 1. Galen—Juvenile literature. 2. Human anatomy—Biography—Juvenile literature. I. Title.
R126.G8Y68 2010
611.0092—dc22
[B]

                          2008029633

Printed in the United States of America

10 9 8 7 6 5 4 3 2 1

To Our Readers: We have done our best to make sure all Internet addresses in this book were active
and appropriate when we went to press. However, the author and the publisher have no control over
and assume no liability for the material available on those Internet sites or on other Web sites they may
link to. Any comments or suggestions can be sent by e-mail to comments@enslow.com or to the
address on the back cover.

♻ Enslow Publishers, Inc., is committed to printing our books on recycled paper. The paper in every
book contains 10% to 30% post-consumer waste (PCW). The cover board on the outside of each book
contains 100% PCW. Our goal is to do our part to help young people and the environment too!

Illustration Credits: Anatomical Design/Shutterstock Images LLC, p. 57; Danilo Ascione/
Shutterstock Images LLC, p. 43; Enslow Publishers, Inc., p. 80; Geoffrey Lawrence/
Shutterstock Images LLC, p. 54; Granger Collection, New York, pp. 1, 28, 45, 82, 101, 102,
107; History of Medicine Division, National Library of Medicine, p. 99; Kim Austin/ Enslow
Publishers, Inc., pp. 66, 106; Life Art Image © 1998 Lippincott Williams & Wilkins, all
rights reserved, p. 55; Mary Evans Picture Library/Everett Collection, p. 16; Robert A.
Thom/ courtesy of the History of Medicine Division, National Library of Medicine, pp. 70,
84; Science Source/courtesy Photo Researchers, Inc., p. 8; SPL/Photo Researchers, Inc., p.
23; Sumbul/iStock International Inc., p. 12; Visual Arts Library (London)/Alamy, p. 105;
Xyno/iStock International Inc., p. 13.

Cover Illustration: The Granger Collection, New York.

CONTENTS

Introduction: A Visit to the Doctor

JIMMY'S MOTHER HAS BROUGHT HIM TO the doctor. "Jimmy has been sick for days," she says. "He throws up everything he eats. He goes to the bathroom a lot, too."

"And my stomach hurts," Jimmy adds. "And I feel hot. I think I have a fever."

"Well, let's take a look at you," the doctor says. She holds Jimmy's wrist for a minute, staring intently at the second hand on her watch. "Yes, your pulse is pretty fast. That means your heart is working harder than usual. That could go with having a fever."

The doctor puts a thermometer in Jimmy's mouth to take his temperature. "You do indeed have a fever," she agrees. "Three degrees higher than normal." She uses a stethoscope to listen to Jimmy's heart and lungs. "Everything sounds good there," she says.

"Now, tell me, Jimmy," the doctor goes on. "Where did you go and what were you doing just before you got sick?"

"We went to a barbecue at Uncle Bill's house," Jimmy says.

"What did you eat there?"

"Ribs cooked with Uncle Bill's special sauce, an' potato salad, an' Aunt Tillie's cherry pie for dessert."

"Did you eat the same things, Mrs. Morrison?" the doctor asks Jimmy's mother.

"Well, I skipped the potato salad. I don't like eggs, and Aunt Tillie always puts lots of hard-boiled eggs in her salad. She uses too much mayonnaise, too."

"I see. And did your picnic happen on time?"

"No, we had to wait around for ages," Jimmy says. "Aunt Tillie had everything set out and ready, but Uncle Bill just couldn't get the barbecue going."

"Okay," the doctor says, "I can make a guess about what's wrong with you. Most likely, while you were waiting for Uncle Bill and the barbecue, some germs in Aunt Tillie's salad had time to grow. After you ate the salad, they made you sick. I want to take a sample of your blood to make sure. We'll send it to a laboratory, and someone there will look at it under a microscope and try to spot the germs. But meanwhile, I can give you some medicine that will put your digestive system back in balance. Then it will work the way it should again. You should start to feel better in a day or two."

Jimmy and his doctor might not know it, but many of the things the doctor did were the same things a good doctor would have done two thousand years ago. She checked Jimmy's pulse, feeling his heartbeat in his wrist. She asked him about what he had been doing and eating before he became sick. She used what she knew about the organs inside his body to help her guess what was wrong with him. She told Jimmy what had made him sick and how long his illness would

Galen, a Greek physician who lived in the second century A.D., was the authority on medical knowledge in the Western world for more than fifteen hundred years.

probably last. She chose a treatment that would restore the natural balance of substances in his body.

A Greek doctor named Galen put all those ideas—and many more—into writing in the second century A.D. He gathered together most of the medical knowledge that had been obtained in the Western world up to that time. He also extended that knowledge by discovering more than anyone had known before about the inside of the body. He wrote that doctors had to understand how the body works if they wanted to treat sick people successfully. Doctors learned medicine from Galen's writings for more than fifteen hundred years. His ideas still shape what physicians do today.

1

A DREAM CAREER

PERGAMUM WAS A THRILLING PLACE TO grow up. When Galen was born there in September of A.D. 129, this beautiful city was the capital of the Roman Empire's province of Asia. (That province was actually a peninsula on the western coast of the continent of Asia, sometimes called Asia Minor. The Asian part of Turkey occupies it now. A Turkish town called Bergama stands on the site of Pergamum today and preserves the ancient city's name.) Rome had ruled this area for almost three hundred years, but its people and culture were proudly Greek.

People from all over the empire came to Pergamum. Built in a lush valley where three rivers met, 15 miles from the Aegean Sea, the city was a busy and wealthy trading spot.

Pergamum also had a long history as a center of learning. More than three hundred years before Galen's birth, its library had almost rivaled the one in Alexandria, Egypt, which was the largest library in the ancient world. Indeed, one story said that the ruler of Alexandria in those days grew so jealous of the Pergamum library that he would not let papyrus, the Egyptian reed from which paper was made, be sent to the city. That did not stop the Pergamenes. They simply turned animal skins into a paperlike material and wrote on those. This material was later called parchment, a word that comes from the city's name. Papyrus was good for making scrolls, the rolled-up form in which most documents were kept in those days. Parchment, though, was better for making flat-paged books. We may thus owe books at least partly to Pergamum.

Visitors to Pergamum admired the shrine of Zeus, the Greek father of the gods, in the highest part of the city. The temple that meant the most

These are the ruins of a second-century health center called Allianoi, near Galen's hometown of Pergamum (modern-day Bergama, Turkey).

to many, though, was built around a sacred spring outside the city walls. It belonged to Asclepius, the Greek god of healing. Sick people slept in the temple after praying that Asclepius would come to them in their dreams. They hoped that the god would tell them what was wrong with them and how they could regain their health. The temple's priests also gave the people whatever medical treatment they could.

A Devoted Father

The temple of Asclepius was rebuilt and expanded when Galen was a boy. His father,

Nicon, may have helped in the project. Nicon was an architect, or designer of buildings. A wealthy man, he also owned several estates and farms.

Galen admired his father tremendously. He later called Nicon "extremely slow to anger, as well as . . . just, decent, and generous."[1] He did not like his mother, though. He wrote that she argued with his father all the time. She became

The staff of Asclepius is still used as a symbol of medicine. It is often confused with the caduceus, the winged staff with two snakes intertwined around it, which is the emblem of Mercury (the Greek Hermes), the messenger of the Roman gods.

upset over little things and bit her servants when they made her angry.

Perhaps Nicon chose his son's name, which means "calm" or "serene" in Greek, in the hope that Galen would not act like his wife. Galen seems to have had the same hope. "When I saw . . . the nobility of my father's conduct side by side with the shameful passions of my mother," he wrote later, "I made up my mind to love and cleave to the former behavior."[2] All his life, Galen warned against giving in to emotion.

Nicon spent much time and money on educating Galen, his only child. He picked out the boy's teachers personally and even did some of the work himself. He taught Galen about astronomy and geometry, for instance. This instruction gave Galen a great respect for mathematics and exact measurement. As an adult, he tried to bring this exactness into medicine. Galen may also have learned about doing experiments from Nicon. For instance, Nicon tried storing jugs of wine at different temperatures to see which lasted the longest.

Galen loved learning as much as his father hoped he would. According to one story, he told other children that he would rather read than play. By the time he was thirteen years old, he had already written three books of his own.

A Change of Plans

When Galen was fourteen, Nicon began taking him to hear lectures by famous philosophers. Philosophers are professional thinkers, a little like college professors today. (*Philosopher* means "lover of wisdom" in Greek.) There were four main types or "schools" of philosophy in Galen's day, and he heard speakers from each. Nicon told him to learn from all of them but not to become devoted to any one point of view. This advice, too, Galen took to heart.

Nicon probably hoped that Galen himself would become a philosopher, or perhaps take a role in government. In 145, though, when Galen was sixteen, Nicon had a dream that changed his plans for his son. In his dream, the god Asclepius told him that Galen should become a physician.

Galen and his father attended lectures by renowned philosophers, which were probably very similar to this scene of Plato (c. 428–347 b.c.) teaching his students at the Academy in Athens. Plato was one of the most influential thinkers of the Western world, a distinction Galen would also possess centuries later in the field of medicine.

Like most people of their day, Nicon and Galen believed that some dreams foretold the future. After this dream, therefore, Galen started going to the temple of Asclepius to learn about treating sick people. He also studied with a doctor named Satyrus. Satyrus recommended dissecting, or cutting up, the bodies of animals to see the organs and other parts hidden inside. This made Galen curious about anatomy, the structure of the body.

Travel and Study

Nicon died in 148 or 149. His death must have made nineteen-year-old Galen very sad, since father and son had been so close. It also made him rich. Most men who wanted to be physicians learned their work just by watching and helping older doctors. Galen, though, wanted more— and could afford it. He decided to travel to other cities to study with famous doctors there. He also planned to go on with his studies in philosophy.

Galen went first to the city of Smyrna (now Izmir, Turkey). There he wrote his earliest surviving book, which described the movement of the heart and lungs. He then went on to Corinth (in Greece) and finally to Alexandria, which he had heard was the best place to study medicine. He stayed there for five years, beginning around 152. During all his years of study, Galen later claimed, "I repudiated [gave up] all pleasure. . . . Instead I spent all my time in the study of medical practice. . . . I have gone without sleep at night in order to examine the treasures left to us by the Ancients."[3]

Alexandria was certainly a fine place to do that. Galen probably wished, though, that he could have been in the city four hundred years before. Alexandrian doctors of that time had studied human anatomy openly. In most ancient places and times, including Galen's own day, cutting up dead human bodies was against the law. People believed that the spirits of the dead could not find rest if their bodies were harmed. For a few decades, however, Alexandrian kings had allowed the bodies of executed criminals to be dissected. There were even reports that the king had let living criminals be cut open. Some historians think this was not true, however.

Anatomy Pioneers

Galen learned about two physicians who had lived in Alexandria during that time. Their names were Herophilus and Erasistratus. Most of what was known about the inside of the human body had come from their work.

Following the ideas of the ancient philosopher Aristotle, some doctors believed that nerves and thoughts came from the heart. Herophilus and Erasistratus, though, said that both came from the brain. Herophilus also showed that there were two kinds of nerves. One kind helped the body move. The other carried sensations from the body to the brain.

The two men had also studied the heart and the pipelike vessels that came from it. Erasistratus, for instance, showed that the human heart contained four valves. These valves were like doors that swing open to let blood flow in one direction. If the blood tried to wash back the other way, the valves slammed shut and stopped it. Because of these valves, blood moving through the heart could follow only one path.

Both Herophilus and Erasistratus showed that blood vessels, like nerves, existed in two types. They called one kind *arteries* and the other *veins*. Both agreed that veins carried blood through the body. Herophilus perhaps thought that arteries did, too. Erasistratus, however, said that arteries contained only air—or rather an airlike substance called *pneuma* [NOO-muh], which he believed was just as vital to the body as blood.

Galen wrote later that he found Alexandria disappointing. Doctors there could no longer cut up human corpses. They had to use animals instead. The only human parts Galen could study were some skeletons that earlier physicians had prepared. The skeletons taught him about the bones of the body, at least.

The Father of Medicine

Galen also learned about sects or "schools" of medicine. There were several of these, just as in philosophy. Each had different ideas about health and disease. The one Galen liked the best centered on the writings of Hippocrates (hip-AH-cra-teez), the so-called Father of Medicine. Hippocrates was supposed to have lived on the Greek island of Cos, off the western coast of Asia Minor, between about 460 and 370 B.C. In fact, though, historians then—and now—knew almost nothing about his life for certain. He had become a legendary, almost magical, figure. Some people said he was descended from Asclepius himself.

Galen read a group of about seventy writings that Hippocrates was supposed to have written. Even in Galen's day, people guessed that several different authors had actually created these works. No one was sure which ones—if any—had come from Hippocrates himself. (Some modern historians doubt whether any of Hippocrates' own writings survived.) In spite of this, the writings created a consistent picture of what sickness was and how doctors should treat it.

Unlike most physicians before them and in

their own time, Hippocrates and his followers did not believe that sickness was caused by gods or evil spirits. Instead, they said, it came from natural changes in the body. When a person was healthy, all the substances in the body were in balance. In illness, the balance was destroyed. The doctor's job was to restore it by adding or subtracting substances.

The body's balance could be damaged by changes in a person's surroundings, the followers of Hippocrates said. Because of this, a doctor had to observe carefully and ask many questions to find out what had made a person sick. He had to look for changes in the weather or in what the person ate or drank, for instance. Then, using all he had learned about the patient and the patient's environment, the doctor *diagnosed* the patient's disease. He said what kind of sickness it was and what had caused it. He also gave a *prognosis,* or prediction of what would happen as the illness ran its course. He prescribed drugs, changes in diet, or other treatments that would bring back health.

Galen liked the commonsense approach of Hippocrates and his students. Although Galen never lost his belief in Asclepius, he thought that doctors could learn more about disease and treatment by studying nature than by praying to gods. He liked the Hippocratic idea that both observing and reasoning were important parts of medicine. Hippocrates became Galen's hero.

Hippocrates, the "Father of Medicine." His assumptions that diseases and cures came from nature, not the gods, and that a physician could treat a patient using knowledge obtained from experience or medical texts still form the basis of modern medicine.

The only thing his idol had lacked, Galen decided, was knowledge about the inside of the body. The Hippocratic writings said almost nothing about the body's structure or how its different parts worked. By learning and writing about these things, Galen felt that he could complete the work of the man that he admired so much.

Galen's First Job

Galen went back to Pergamum in the autumn of 157. He probably thought he had learned all he could by traveling. He may have been homesick as well. He revisited Pergamum from time to time all through his life, and he gave the city many compliments in his writings. For instance, he wrote that honey harvested from its hills was the best he had ever tasted.

By this time, Galen was almost twenty-eight years old. He had had twelve years of study, far more than other doctors of his time. He was more than ready to call himself a physician.

The temple of Asclepius in Pergamum owned

a troop of gladiators, professional fighters who staged battles to entertain visitors on holidays. This sort of contest was common in the Roman Empire. People flocked to gladiator contests as they do to football or soccer matches today. Galen learned that the troop needed a new doctor, and he applied for the job.

Galen knew that only the most skilled physician would be hired. Gladiators often received terrible wounds, and the owners of troops like this tried hard to help their men recover and stay healthy. For one thing, the best gladiators were worth a great deal of money. They were the sports stars of their day.

The temple's chief priest would choose the gladiators' doctor. Galen showed the priest a new dressing, or covering, that he had invented to use on certain kinds of wounds. He also cut open the abdomen of a monkey and showed how he would treat this kind of wound. His treatments worked better than those of the physicians competing with him, even though he was much younger than they were, and he won the post.

Galen, who loved to brag about his successes, wrote later that the high priest said, "I have seen that this man has devoted more time to learning this science [medicine] than any of the Elders of the physicians. . . . He never ceases on any day or at any hour to train himself in something useful. Besides, . . . his practical performance . . . more correctly indicates skill in this art, than the many years of the Elders."[4]

Physician to the Gladiators

Dealing with the wide range of wounds that the gladiators received in different kinds of contests was a challenge for Galen. Sometimes the gladiators fought each other with swords. Sometimes one man had a sword while the other had only a net and a short, three-pronged spear called a trident. At other times, the gladiators battled each other while riding on horses or in war chariots. They might fight lions or other wild animals as well. Each type of contest had its own risks.

Galen treated his fighters with both surgery

and drugs. He did not like to use surgery, but when it was required, his knowledge of anatomy kept him from making mistakes that other doctors made. Some physicians tried to sew separate muscles or tendons (strong bands of tissue that tie muscles to bones) together, for instance, but Galen knew better. Those parts were not joined in the healthy body, he said, so they should not be joined in a wounded one. For the same reason, he knew not to sew muscles to the skin or flesh near the edges of a wound. If a surgeon did so, the wound would soon pull open again.

Galen tried to stop bleeding by raising the injured part and pressing on the wound. If he saw spurting blood vessels, he tied them shut with silk. He also put substances on the wound to slow the bleeding. These included spiderwebs, egg white, and even rabbit fur. Some surgeons poured hot oil or harsh drugs on wounds, but Galen used milder ones that would not damage the flesh. He bandaged the wounds with linen cloth soaked in wine.[5]

In addition to helping the gladiators, Galen realized that his work was giving him the practical experience he needed to round out his years of book learning. He might not be able to dissect human corpses, but living men cut up almost as completely were brought to him every day. He had chances to study muscles, nerves, blood vessels, and even organs such as the liver

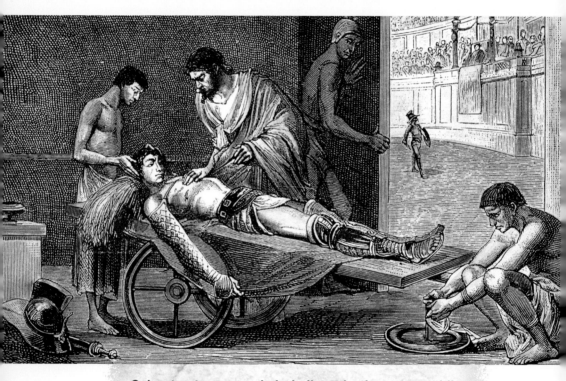

Galen treats a wounded gladiator in the arena, while the bloody battles continue right outside the door.

and intestines while trying to sew up their wounds. He also learned what kinds of diet and exercise kept athletes healthy and strong.

Galen worked hard at his job and was proud of what he accomplished. He wrote later that only two gladiators died during his first year as the troop's doctor, while sixteen had died the year before. He may have been exaggerating his success, as he sometimes did. The priests of Asclepius must have liked his work, though, because they rehired him each year for several years. In one of those years, Galen said, none of his patients died, "even though each suffered grave [serious] and multiple wounds."[6]

First Among Physicians

IN THE SUMMER OF 162, WHEN HE WAS thirty-two years old, Galen decided to travel again. His writings hint that he left Pergamum partly to escape a local war or political unrest. Very likely his main reason, though, was that he wanted more out of life than even that fine city could offer him.

People of Galen's day usually viewed physicians merely as skilled workmen. (Some women cared for the sick, especially helping other women in childbirth, but they were not normally counted as physicians.) Doctors were like the carpenters who built furniture, or the blacksmiths who made iron tools. Some stayed in one place all their lives, while others rode from town to town, treating patients where they found them.[1]

Galen felt he was much more than that. He had grown up among wealthy and educated people. He had read and studied far more than most other physicians. He was trained in philosophy as well as medicine. He wanted to share his ideas with the world.

The best place to do that was in the glittering capital of the empire: Rome itself. Galen knew that he would be far from the first Greek doctor to move to that city. Indeed, as P. N. Singer, who translated and edited a collection of Galen's writings in English, put it, "Medicine was essentially a Greek import to Rome."[2] For several hundred years before Galen went there, the personal physicians of most Roman high society families had come from Greece.

Indeed, most educated Romans of Galen's time admired many aspects of Greek culture. They often spoke and read Greek as well as their own language, Latin. People used Latin for business, law, government, and everyday speech, but many books of science and philosophy were written in Greek. Galen expected to feel right at home in the capital.

Setting up a Practice

Once he reached Rome, Galen rented a fine house and set about letting Rome know that an expert physician had arrived. Several wealthy men whom he had known in Pergamum lived there. He called on these acquaintances, and some became his patients.

One of the first well-known Romans whom Galen treated was an elderly philosopher named Eudemus. Eudemus, who may have been one of Galen's teachers when Galen was young, happened to live next door to him in Rome. The winter after Galen moved in, Eudemus developed a fever that returned every few days. The fever almost surely was caused by a disease now called malaria, which was common in the Roman world at that time.

Doctors today know that malaria is caused by a tiny parasite that lives in the blood. Galen could not guess that, but through experience and reading, he knew the pattern that the disease usually followed. He startled Eudemus by telling him exactly when his fever would rise and fall. None of the other doctors treating him had been able to do that. Furthermore, the other doctors said that Eudemus would surely die, but Galen gave him a medicine that cured him. The other physicians had used a similar drug, but Galen said that they had given it too soon. He told them it would work only after the disease had reached a certain stage.

Eudemus was so impressed with Galen's prognosis and treatment that he told all his friends about it. He even compared Galen to Apollo, the Greek god of the sun. (Apollo was the father of Asclepius and held to be a healer himself.) Eudemus's friends included high government officials and members of the court of the new co-emperors, the brothers Marcus Aurelius Antoninus and Lucius Verus. Indeed, Galen wrote, thanks to Eudemus, "almost all the social and intellectual leaders of Rome" soon heard about the marvelous new physician.[3]

Startling Demonstrations

Another powerful new friend of Galen's was Flavius Boethius, who had been a consul (an important government official). After Galen cured Boethius's wife of a bleeding disorder, Boethius introduced the physician to emperor Marcus Aurelius himself.

Boethius also thought of another way that Galen could make himself known. Galen's success with Eudemus and other wealthy Romans had made other high society physicians very jealous, and they were spreading rumors that Galen did not know as much as he said he did. Boethius suggested that Galen give public demonstrations to prove his skill. Other doctors had put on similar performances, and people attended them for both learning and entertainment.

Galen decided that Boethius's idea was a good one. He had made some exciting discoveries about anatomy while experimenting on animals in Pergamum. He could repeat some of those experiments as demonstrations, he thought. He would begin with facts that everyone agreed about. Then he would use the logic he had learned as a philosopher to lead his audience to new understandings about the body.

Soon after he treated Eudemus, Galen began giving demonstrations at a spot called the Temple of Peace. Philosophers and other intellectuals often met there to talk and argue. Galen's demonstrations proved to be very popular. Even the emperors' uncle and son-in-law came to some of them.

Most of Galen's demonstrations used living animals. (Experimenting on live animals in this way is called *vivisection*.) Such experiments would seem terribly cruel today, but neither Galen nor his audience saw anything wrong with them. After all, Romans were used to watching men kill wild animals—and each other—in the arena during gladiator contests. Galen's actions probably did not seem much different.

Galen performed one of his most famous demonstrations on a pig. In humans, speaking expresses thoughts. Most doctors of the time believed that the heart controlled both thoughts and the voice, just as Aristotle had said. Galen, however, agreed with Herophilus and Erasistratus that thoughts came from the brain and were carried by nerves. He had found that nerves controlled the voice, too. He used the unlucky pig to prove it.

The idea for this demonstration came from experiments Galen had done in Pergamum. While studying the nerves and muscles that control breathing, he had found a tiny pair of nerves that went to the larynx. This boxlike structure in the throat produces the voice by changing the flow of air that comes from the lungs through the windpipe.

Galen used his demonstration to show what these two nerves did. First, he cut the pig's skin in several places. The animal, of course, squealed loudly. Then Galen cut the nerves leading to the larynx. The pig still thrashed in pain, but its squealing suddenly stopped. The group of connected nerves Galen had found are still named after him.[4]

Arguing About Medicine

Galen also held public debates with leaders of different medical sects. Such arguments were another common activity in the Temple of Peace. Doctors used them to present their views on medicine. The debating physicians also tried to impress their hearers and persuade them to become new patients.

Galen, too, no doubt used the debates as a form of advertisement. He also used them to show how his experiments on anatomy or his study of ancient authors, especially Hippocrates, proved that certain beliefs of his opponents were wrong. He later repeated some of these arguments in his books.

Galen seemed to like arguing even more than other doctors did. When he thought an opponent's views were foolish, he did not hesitate to say so. There is no report that he ever bit anyone, but perhaps he was more like his mother than he would have wanted to admit.

The three main medical sects in Rome were the Dogmatists, the Empiricists, and the Methodists. The Dogmatists thought that doctors should take most of their ideas from famous physicians of the past. They said that careful, logical thinking was more important than observation. They used theories about the body to guide them in guessing the causes of disease and working out treatments.

The Empiricists, on the other hand, thought book learning was worthless. They saw no use for theories about anatomy or disease. Doctors should learn medicine, they said, by observing sick people and noticing which treatments helped or cured them. They could then use those same treatments each time they saw similar symptoms, or visible signs of illness.

Galen thought both of these groups were partly right and partly wrong. He said that a good physician should use both reasoning and observation, book study and practical training.

He believed that doctors should learn theories first, then test them by observing and experimenting.

Galen respected the Dogmatists and the Empiricists, even when he disagreed with them. He did not feel the same way about the Methodists. (This group had no connection with the later Christian church that used the same name.) The Methodists reduced medicine to such a simple system that they claimed a person could learn it in a mere six months. They thought that all diseases were due to tiny body openings called pores being either too open or too tightly closed. Galen said that their ideas were both foolish and dangerous.

Galen's bragging and sharp tongue in the debates made other physicians dislike him. His continued success in Roman society also made them more jealous of him than ever. Eudemus finally warned him that, if his rivals could not drive him out of the city, they might try to poison him. Galen wrote later that this fear for his life was the reason he left Rome in the summer of

166 and went back to Pergamum. He crept away secretly, "like a runaway slave," he said.[5] He may also have been trying to escape a disease epidemic that was just starting to sweep through Rome.

Treating an Emperor

Galen was not able to stay away for long. Marcus Aurelius and Lucius Verus were preparing to attack Germanic tribes that had been crossing the Danube River to raid Roman provinces in northern Italy. The Roman troops were camped at a town called Aquileia. Toward the end of 168, the emperors ordered Galen to join them there as a military doctor. He did not dare to say no.

While at Aquileia, Galen had a chance to treat Marcus Aurelius himself.[6] One night the emperor had a stomachache and diarrhea. His other doctors decided that he was coming down with a fever, but Galen thought they were wrong. He concluded, instead, that the ruler had eaten food that was making him sick. He recommended putting a sort of heating pad, made of red wool soaked in a warm, sweet-smelling ointment, on Marcus's abdomen. He also told the emperor to drink wine with pepper sprinkled in it. Marcus Aurelius followed his advice and soon felt better. Galen wrote that the emperor called him a "very enlightened gentleman" and "first among physicians and unique among philosophers."[7]

Shortly afterward, a new disease outbreak forced the emperors to return to Rome. Lucius Verus died on the way home, leaving Marcus Aurelius as sole emperor. Galen and the army followed more slowly, after spending what G. E. R. Lloyd, a professor of classics (the study of ancient Greek and Latin writings) and early science at England's Cambridge University, called a "miserable winter" in camp.[8]

Productive Years

Marcus Aurelius was ready to return to battle later in 169, and he expected Galen to go with him. Galen, however, told the emperor that, like his father long ago, he had been visited by

Asclepius in a dream. The god had told him to stay in Rome. Instead of following Marcus Aurelius, Galen asked to be the physician for eight-year-old Commodus, the emperor's son and heir. The emperor agreed.

During the next six years, Commodus traveled from one imperial country house to another. Galen was part of the court that went with him. The boy had few health problems, though, so he and Galen probably did not see much of each other. Instead, Galen spent most of his time writing. He had been an author all his life, but composing books now became his main activity. He did some of his most important work during this time. For example, he wrote *On the Uses of Parts,* which described what he knew about the functions of different parts of the human body.

Galen also continued his research on anatomy during these years. He dissected and experimented on many dead and living animals. He seldom gave demonstrations or took part in debates anymore, however. He was too successful

A statue of Marcus Aurelius stands in Rome, Italy. Galen served as a personal physician to both Marcus Aurelius and the emperor's son, Commodus.

to need to advertise, and he had concluded that these performances brought him more trouble than they were worth.

Imperial Physician

Marcus Aurelius returned to Rome in 175 and made Galen one of his personal physicians. The emperor was a philosopher and a writer, just as Galen was, and the two may have become friends. They certainly must have had some interesting conversations. The emperor never mentioned Galen in his own writings, though, so perhaps he and Galen were not as close as Galen liked to suggest.[9]

Friend or not, Galen seems to have remained in the imperial household for most, if not all, of the rest of his own long life. After Marcus Aurelius died in 180, Galen became a physician to the new emperor, Commodus. Unlike Marcus Aurelius, Commodus was not a good or popular emperor. He was murdered in 192. Galen stayed in court to attend the emperors who followed.

This parade of emperors were far from Galen's

Galen wrote hundreds of books during his lifetime.
Copies and translations of his writings had to be done
painstakingly by hand by scribes like the ones
depicted in this wood engraving.

only patients. He wrote that he treated both rich and poor people, never charging a fee. (He did accept gifts from wealthy patients, though.) He even gave medical advice by mail. People from as far away as Iberia (Spain) and Asia heard about his skill and wrote to ask for his help.

Galen lived a long life, but historians are not sure how long. For many years, most believed that he had died around 200, when he was seventy years old. Newly discovered Arabic writings, however, suggest that he probably lived until around 217.[10] He would have been eighty-seven years old in that year—an amazingly long span of life for his time. Historians are not sure whether he died in Rome or returned to spend his last years in his hometown, Pergamum.

A Wide-Ranging Author

Galen's life was as productive as it was lengthy. He appears to have written several hundred books. Some were lost in 192 because of a fire that swept through the Temple of Peace, where he stored many of his manuscripts. The Greek editions of others vanished, but the works still exist in translations into Latin, Arabic, or Syraic (another ancient Middle Eastern language). At least half of Galen's writings survived in their original Greek, however—enough to fill twenty thick volumes when German scholar Karl G. Kühn edited and translated them into Latin in the 1820s and 1830s. (Kühn's books include both the Greek and the Latin texts, as well as some translations of Galen by earlier scholars.) Texts by Galen (including some additional manuscripts that have been discovered since Kühn's day) make up a major part of the ancient Greek medical writings that exist today.

Not surprisingly, most of Galen's books were about medicine. Some described his discoveries in anatomy and physiology (how different parts of the body work). Others told doctors and medical students how to understand disease, treat patients, and make drugs.

Galen also wrote books that explained and praised the ideas of his hero, Hippocrates, as Galen understood them. He felt that he was completing or perfecting the work of Hippocrates and other early doctors. He wrote: "I have done as much for medicine as [the emperor] Trajan did for the Roman Empire when he built bridges and roads through Italy. It is I, and I alone, who have revealed the true path of medicine. . . . Hippocrates . . . prepared the way, but I have made it passable."[11]

In addition, Galen wrote criticisms of the teachings of famous physicians and medical sects, both from his own time and earlier. Many of these other doctors' own writings were later lost. All we know about them today, therefore, is what Galen wrote. Galen also shaped later physicians' understanding of better-known figures, especially Hippocrates. Galen's works, in fact, summarize most of the teachings of Greek and Roman medicine that have survived.

Philosophy was just as important as medicine to Galen, so he wrote books on that subject, too. Some parts of his books tell how he thought people should live. For instance, he said that most troubles come from poor decisions made because of strong passions, or emotions, such as anger and greed. Such decisions can lead to illness, he wrote, and so can the emotions themselves.

Galen criticized the laziness and love of luxury that he saw all around him in Rome. He told people not to care about fame, money, or possessions. He used his own life as an example of the way he believed a philosopher should live.

In addition to medicine and philosophy, Galen wrote about basic ideas in natural science, such as the nature of matter. He disagreed with thinkers who believed that both living and nonliving matter were made out tiny particles called atoms. He also wrote books about the Greek language and other subjects.

Some of Galen's books were partly about himself. No single book describes his life in detail, but many of his writings include comments about his life and experiences. He also published two lists of the books he had written and when he wrote them. He did this, he said, because other people were taking advantage of his fame by writing books and claiming that they were his.

Finally, Galen's books contain interesting details about life in the Roman Empire in his time. "He had a sharp eye, wherever he traveled," writes Vivian Nutton, a British historian who is an expert on Galen.[12] Because Galen wrote so much about himself and his surroundings, historians know far more about this remarkable man than they do about most other ancient scientists and other writers.

3

EXPLORING THE BODY

BEFORE GALEN, FEW DOCTORS HAD TRIED to learn the structure of the inside of the body and the way that different body parts worked. At most, they made guesses based on philosophical ideas. Some claimed that anything a doctor could not find out by observing a patient could not be known—and probably was not worth knowing.

Galen said they were mistaken. Over and over, he wrote that doctors could understand what went wrong with the body in disease only if they knew how all its parts worked when they were healthy. In *On Anatomical Procedures*, he wrote: "What could be more useful to a physician for the treatment of war-wounds, for extraction of missiles [objects shot into the flesh], for excision [removal] of bones . . . than to know accurately all the parts of the arms and legs. . . . If a man is ignorant of the position of a vital nerve, muscle, artery or important vein, he is more likely to be responsible for the death, than for the saving, of his patients."[1]

Learning From Animals

Building on the work of pioneers such as Herophilus and Erasistratus, Galen set out to discover facts about the body that physicians needed to know. Since dissecting or experimenting on humans, even dead ones, was against the law, he had to use animals. He hoped that the animals he chose would have the same basic body structure as humans. In many ways they did—but some features were different. Because he did not know about these differences, Galen made some important mistakes in his guesses about human anatomy. Still, he learned more about the structure of the body than anyone who had come before him—or anyone who would come after him for almost fourteen hundred years.

Galen's favorite animal to dissect was the so-called Barbary ape. He said that it was more like a human than any other animal he knew. This creature is not really an ape, but rather a type of African monkey known today as the macaque. (Scientists still often use a closely related kind of monkey, the rhesus macaque, in their experiments.) Galen also cut up cattle, horses, pigs, dogs, sheep, and many other kinds of animals. Once he even dissected the heart of an elephant—before cooks took it away for the emperor's dinner.[2]

Galen said that other doctors and medical students also should learn anatomy by dissecting animals. He wrote a book called *On Anatomical Procedures* that told them how to do this. (It was so accurate that modern doctors at Johns Hopkins Medical School in Baltimore, Maryland, used it to dissect the arm of a rhesus monkey and reported that it provided better directions than their current textbooks.)

Students could understand the body's structure, he said, only if they saw it for themselves: "If anyone wishes to observe the works of Nature, he should put his trust not in books on anatomy but in his own eyes."[3] He also wrote several other books on the anatomy of particular parts of the body and on the way different parts are changed by sickness.

A macaque monkey, known in Galen's time as a Barbery ape. Galen dissected these animals to learn more about human anatomy. Humans and monkeys share many similarities in their anatomies, but the differences that exist led to mistakes in Galen's conclusions.

Begin With Bones

When learning about the body, Galen said, students should start with the bones.

"What tent-poles are to tents, and walls to houses, so to animals is their bony structure," he wrote in *On Anatomical Procedures*.[4] He wrote a separate book, called *Bones for Beginners*, to guide them.

Galen said that if students could do so, they should go to Alexandria, as he had done, to study human bones. "The physicians in that country accompany the instruction they give to their students

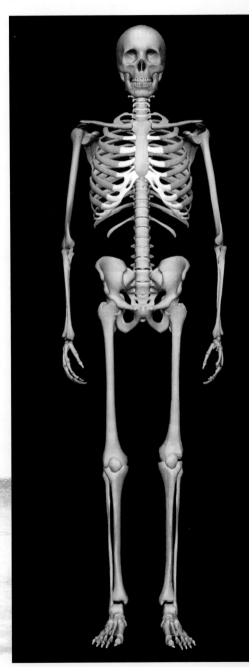

A three-dimensional frontal view of the human skeleton. Galen believed that studying the bones was the first step in understanding anatomy.

with opportunities for personal inspection" of human skeletons, he wrote.[5] If such travel was impossible, they should learn about bones by dissecting Barbary apes and other animals. Then, if they ever had a chance to see human skeletons, they would be able to "easily recognize and remember everything."[6]

Galen himself took every chance he could to learn about human bones, he said. For instance, he looked at a skeleton that a flood had washed out of its grave. He also examined the remains of a robber who had been killed and left by the roadside. He told students that they, too, should watch for such opportunities.

Nerves and Muscles

Some of Galen's most important discoveries concerned the brain and nerves. His experiment with the voice was only one of them. He traced nerves coming down from the brain and out of the spinal cord, the rope of nerves covered by the backbone. He showed that if he cut nerves coming from the spinal cord, certain parts of the animal could no longer move. Cutting the nerves in different places paralyzed different parts of the animal's body. He even noticed that if he cut across half of the cord, only one side of the body would be paralyzed.

Galen also showed how nerves and muscles work together to let animals breathe. He showed that the diaphragm (DI-uh-fram) and other chest muscles make the open space inside the chest expand when an animal breathes in. This expansion pulls air into the lungs.

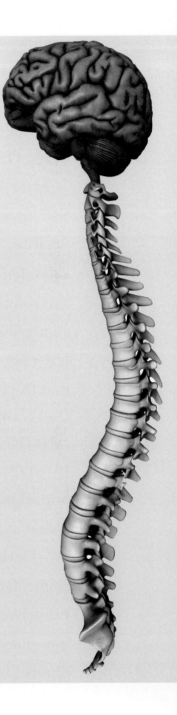

This diagram shows the brain and the spine. The spinal cord is protected by the backbone. Galen discovered that the brain, not the heart, controlled movement through nerves that extended into different parts of the body.

(Before Galen did his experiments, people thought that, instead, the filling lungs forced the chest to swell out.) In breathing out, the muscles draw together or contract, pushing air out of the lungs. Galen traced the nerves that control these muscles from the spinal cord. When he cut or tied those nerves, the animal could no longer breathe.

Galen's experiments proved that, as he wrote, "all voluntary movement is produced by muscles controlled by nerves coming from the brain."[7] His discoveries corrected the widely held belief that the power to move came from the heart.

Arteries and Kidneys

In studying blood vessels, Galen corrected an important mistake that Erasistratus had made. Galen agreed with the ancient scientist that the two kinds of vessels—arteries and veins—were connected by other vessels too tiny to see. Erasistratus, though, thought that blood seeped into these vessels only during some kinds of illness. In a healthy person, he said, arteries contained only air. He believed that the bright red blood that shot out when an artery was cut had simply leaked into the wound from the veins. To prove Erasistratus wrong, Galen tied off a short section of the artery of a living animal that was not near any veins. He then cut into the section and showed that blood still poured out.

Galen also used cutting and tying to show how the kidneys and bladder worked. He closed the ureters, the tubes that connect the kidneys to the bladder, by tying pieces of thread around them. When he did this, the bladder no longer filled with urine, as it normally would over time. Instead, the ureters above the thread swelled as urine dripped into them. The ureters below the thread did not swell, showing that urine flowed in only one direction. It had to come from the kidneys, not the bladder as other doctors had thought.

Everything for a Purpose

Galen wrote about physiology, or the way parts of the body work, in several books. *On the Uses of*

Parts is the longest and most famous. This book showed how each body part's structure helps it carry out its function. Galen believed that if doctors understood a part's function or purpose, they could guess its structure. "If it be the arrangement of the eye that you are considering, remember that this is an organ of vision; if it be a foot, that this is an organ of progression [forward movement]," he wrote.[8] The reverse—that structure revealed function—was also true.

Galen wrote *On the Uses of Parts* to explain and prove his belief that Nature makes everything for a purpose. Galen borrowed this idea from Aristotle. Nature, Galen said, had given each part of the body the perfect structure for performing the job it is supposed to do. In his book, Galen pictured Nature as a kind of guiding spirit, almost a god. The book was his hymn of praise to that being, which he admired tremendously. Sometimes his determination to prove that Nature was perfect led him astray. He ignored or even changed evidence that the structure of some parts of the body did not quite fit what he saw as their function.

Three Vital Systems

Galen believed that the liver, the heart, and the brain were the most important organs in the body. Each controlled one of the three systems on which life depended. The liver and veins provided the nutrition needed for growth. The heart and arteries heated the body and gave it energy. The brain and nerves created thought, movement, and the power to learn about the world through the senses.

Life and power for all of these systems, Galen said, came from an invisible substance called *pneuma*. This Greek word can mean "air," but it also has been translated as "spirit." The famous philosopher Plato had written about the same three body systems and said that each had its own "soul." Other thinkers had mentioned the systems and the pneuma, too. Galen, however, expanded on these ideas so much that he made them his own.

Galen wrote that the stomach "cooked" the food that a person ate, turning it into a milky fluid called chyle. The liver attracted, or pulled, the chyle into itself and changed this fluid into a dark-colored, nourishing form of blood. Other parts of the body, in turn, attracted the blood to themselves and were fed by it. (Galen thought that each part of the body had the power to attract to itself all the substances it needed, somewhat the way a magnet pulls iron filings toward itself. This power of attraction, Galen said, was the force that moved blood and other fluids through the body.) Veins carried the dark blood from the liver to the rest of the body. In addition to nourishment, this blood contained a type of pneuma called the natural or physical spirit. Natural pneuma was one of three kinds of pneuma that existed in the body.

Galen knew from his animal dissections that a large vein (now called the vena cava) entered the right side of the heart. He thought that the lungs attracted blood from this vein. The lungs used some of the blood for their nourishment. They combined the natural pneuma in the rest of the blood with the air gained by breathing to make a second kind of pneuma, called vital spirit. Blood containing vital pneuma seeped through the tiny connecting vessels that Erasistratus had mentioned and was attracted into the pulmonary vein (which Galen thought was an artery). When the heart swelled with each beat, it drew blood from this vessel into its left side.

More blood came into the left side of the heart than Galen thought the pulmonary "artery" could carry. He believed that the left part of the heart drew in this blood through tiny openings, or pores, in the wall of muscle that divides the right and left sides of the heart. He could not have seen these pores, because they do not exist. In writing about them, Galen broke his own rule of "believe only what you see with your own eyes." He felt that the pores *had* to be there in order for the heart and blood vessels to work the way he thought they did. He therefore wrote that they *were* there, even though he had not actually observed them. He felt that the logic of his reasoning was proof enough that they were real. He made several other mistakes in his book for the same reason. (Aristotle did the same thing in some of his writings about the anatomy of animals.)

According to Galen, the heart's main job was to heat the blood. The blend of heat and vital pneuma changed the color of the blood from dark to bright red. The body's largest artery, the aorta, is connected to the left side of the heart. Galen said that the aorta attracted this thinner, purer blood into itself, aided by the "collapse" of the heart that occurs during each heartbeat. (What Galen saw as a collapse is actually a contraction, or pulling together, of the heart muscle.) This bright red blood, carried by the aorta and other arteries, spread warmth and energy throughout the body. Galen's animal experiments had shown him proof of these ideas. "If you take any part of the body and bind it tightly, you will see it immediately grow pale and cold, clearly because the heat flowing down through all the parts has been cut off," he wrote.[9]

He had seen the same thing happen when he had tied ligatures, or tourniquets, around the arms or legs of injured gladiators to stop bleeding.

Galen thought that a third kind of pneuma, the psychic pneuma or spirit, was created in the brain when the brain attracted blood into itself. He wrote that this form of pneuma formed partly in a network of blood vessels at the rear base of the brain. He had seen this network, which he called the "wonderful net," when he dissected several kinds of hoofed animals, such as oxen and cattle. He therefore reasoned that it must exist in humans as well, but in fact it does not.

The "wonderful net" of blood vessels combined vital pneuma with air breathed in through the nose to form psychic pneuma, Galen said. He believed that psychic pneuma produced thought. Traveling into the body through the nerves, it also let living things detect their environment through sight, hearing, and

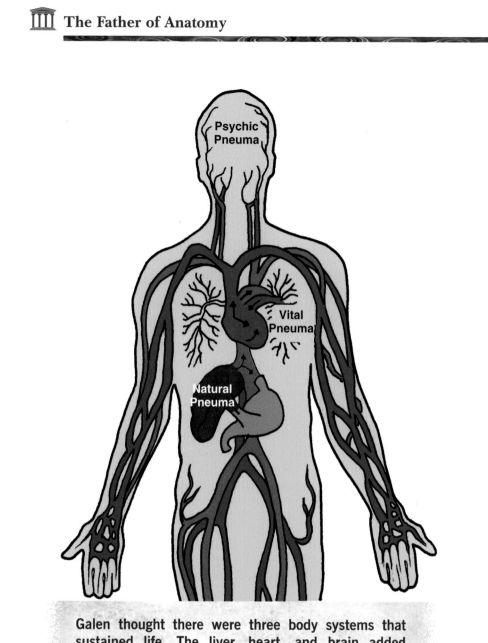

Galen thought there were three body systems that sustained life. The liver, heart, and brain added different kinds of pneuma, or spirits, to the blood. The liver and veins added natural pneuma. The heart and arteries provided vital pneuma. And the brain and nerves supplied psychic pneuma.

other senses. It allowed them to move different parts of their bodies as well.

Even though later scientific discoveries changed many features of Galen's picture of the body, Galen's descriptions of anatomy and physiology were very important. He often corrected earlier writers' mistakes, and he added much information that had not been known before. His writings showed how different parts of the body were related to each other in space and how the parts worked together. Above all, they showed the value of observing and experimenting—making deliberate changes to reveal the workings of nature. Few other Greek or Roman physicians or scientists made as many experiments as Galen did. Modern research in medicine and biology is built on some of the same types of reasoning and experimental techniques that Galen used.

4

HEALING THE SICK

IN HIS STUDIES OF ANATOMY AND physiology, Galen was an ancestor of modern laboratory scientists. He was also a working physician, however. He treated hundreds of patients during his long career. He wrote many books about medicine and the art of being a good doctor. These include *On the Method of Healing*, *On Affected Parts* (describing how different parts of the body are changed by disease), and *On Prognosis*.

Galen believed that, like himself, the best physicians were also philosophers. In fact, he wrote a short book with exactly that title. The three branches of philosophy in Galen's time were physics (which then meant all of science, including biology), logic, and ethics. He said that a good physician would need all of these in his working life. Physics would let the doctor understand the body and nature in general. Logic would help him use his observations of a sick person to figure out what disease the patient had and how to treat it. Ethics would tell him how to behave when interacting with patients and their families.

Visiting Patients

Galen saw patients in his own home, in theirs, or even in public. Unlike some doctors whom he criticized, he made sure that he was clean and well dressed when he was working. He was polite, yet also dignified. He talked to his patients honestly about their condition and what he thought would happen to them. Like Hippocrates, he believed that persuading patients to trust and respect him was an important part of helping them get well.

Galen said that he never charged fees and that he treated poor people as well as wealthy ones. He scolded other doctors for their greed in

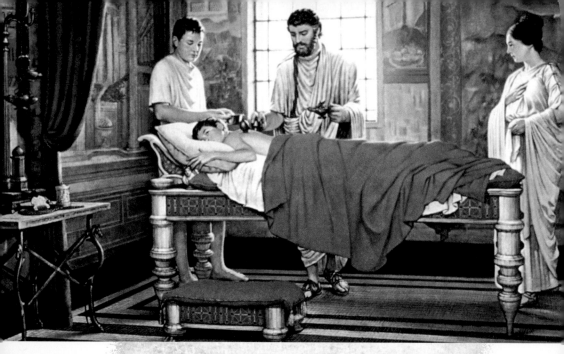

A drawing of Galen using the method of "cupping" to cure a sick boy. A flame heats the cups from the inside, which creates a vacuum, and then they are applied to the skin. The suction draws blood up to the surface of the skin. Practitioners believe this relieves respiratory illnesses, muscle pain, and other ailments.

pursuing rich patients with "a gratifying word or act, a bit of flattery, . . . accompanying them when they go out, staying at their side, escorting them on their homeward journey, amusing them at dinner."[1] He also complained that some doctors tried to impress people "by their expensive clothes and rings, their abundant retinue [troop of assistants and servants] and their flashy silver equipment" instead of their knowledge.[2]

In examining his patients, as in so much else, Galen did what he believed that Hippocrates had taught. He used all his senses to observe the sick people. He wrote that he watched for signs "such as those that appear in the face, the posture the patient adopts in bed, the breathing, . . . presence or absence of headache, . . . prostration [despair] or good spirits."[3] He also felt different parts of his patients' bodies with his hands. He looked at and smelled their urine and bowel movements.

Galen made a point of studying each patient's pulse, the beating of the heart that can be felt in the wrist and certain other places. (He did not realize that the pulse was produced by the heart. He thought it was a movement within the arteries themselves.) He knew that a pulse that was unusually fast or slow, strong or weak, could reflect illness. Other Roman doctors also felt pulses, but Galen wrote that his "most sensitive touch," combined with long experience, let him identify illness from pulses more accurately than anyone else.[4] He wrote twelve books on using the pulse in medicine, describing the many features and variations that it could show.

Hippocrates had told doctors to learn everything they could when talking to their patients, and Galen tried to do so. He asked about the people's daily life, including what they ate and how often they exercised. He found out where they lived and what kind of work they did. He also spoke with the patients' families, friends, and servants. Even objects he saw in their sickrooms sometimes gave him useful hints about the people's illness.

A Medical Detective

Using logic, Galen analyzed all the information he had gathered about a patient to produce a diagnosis and a prognosis. "Once there exists between all the symptoms present a harmony like the voices of a choir in tune, [the doctor] may proceed with confidence," he wrote.[5] In doing this, Galen acted like a detective who studies clues to find out who committed a crime. As in the case of Eudemus, he was often so accurate that people said his work seemed like magic. He once boasted, "I have continued my [medical] practice on until old age, and never . . . have I gone far astray whether in treatment or in prognosis."[6] Galen wrote about people he had diagnosed in *On Prognosis, On Affected Parts,* and other books. These case histories show his "magic" at work.

Like many detectives, Galen sometimes combined observation with what would now be called psychology. He recognized that conditions in the body, such as fever or drunkenness, can affect the mind. He knew that thoughts and feelings can cause changes in the body as well. In fact, he made a specialty of identifying hidden strong emotions—what would now be called stress—as a cause of illness.[7] Changes in the pulse were some of his best clues that someone was feeling stress. (Police still use the pulse to reveal stress when they question suspects attached to lie detectors. These machines record changes in pulse and other signs from the body that are thought to be associated with the stress of lying.)

One stress case that Galen wrote about in *On Prognosis* involved Cyrillus, the young son of Galen's friend Boethius. Like Eudemus, the child had a fever that came and went, but it did not follow the same pattern as Eudemus's. Galen felt sure that this illness was being caused by food that the boy was eating. He prescribed a healthy diet, and Boethius told his wife to make sure Cyrillus ate nothing that was not part of the diet. She watched the boy day and night, even sleeping in his room with the door locked. She made sure that no one visited him.

In spite of these precautions, the fever came back one night. Boethius brought Galen to visit Cyrillus the next day. The boy's pulse told Galen that he no longer had a fever—but he was upset or worried about something. Galen guessed that he had been hiding and secretly eating the kind of food that made him sick. Now he was feeling guilty about it.

After looking around the room and talking to Cyrillus's mother, Galen worked out how the boy was sneaking his forbidden treat. He announced that the child ate the food whenever his mother went to the bathroom, locking the door behind her. Boethius had servants search the room, but no one could find the hidden food. Then, like a magician performing a trick, Galen lifted a shawl that the mother had laid on a chair—the one thing that had not been checked. Sure enough, a piece of bread fell out.

Anatomy Offers Clues

In other cases, Galen let his knowledge of anatomy tell him what was wrong with someone. Some of his conclusions seem amazing even today. For instance, one patient reported that during the previous month or so, he had slowly lost feeling in the last two fingers of one hand. Part of the middle finger had gone numb as well. He could still move the fingers, however. Another doctor had put medicine on the fingers, but that had not helped. Other than this trouble with his hand, the man was healthy.

Galen saw no wound on the man's hand. He suspected that damage to a nerve going to the hand might have caused the problem. He asked the man whether any blow or impact had struck the upper part of his body just before the numbness started. The startled man replied that yes, he had fallen off a cart and landed on his upper back. Galen's dissection of monkeys' nervous systems had given him such a clear picture of the location and function of different nerves that he was able to guess exactly what had happened. Describing this case in *On Affected Parts,* he wrote: "I conjectured [guessed] that, as a result of the blow, there was an inflammation at the spot where the nerves leave the seventh cervical vertebra [the seventh bone down from the skull in the backbone]. . . . The lower end of the last nerve coming from the neck goes to the last two fingers, spreading through the surrounding skin and, in addition, through half of the middle finger."[8]

Galen gave his patient medicine to be placed on his spine instead of on his fingers, and he wrote that the man was cured soon after. It seems unlikely that Galen knew of any drugs that could really heal nerve damage, however. By the time he treated the man, the damage probably was healing by itself.

A Theory of Sickness

Galen wrote that his ideas about what made people sick or healthy, like those about diagnosis and prognosis, came from Hippocrates. He also borrowed some theories from other early physicians and philosophers, such as Aristotle. He combined them into a system all his own.[9]

Galen's system centered on four body fluids called *humors*. According to him, the four were blood, phlegm (FLEM) or mucus, yellow bile, and black bile. All of these except black bile are real fluids, but they do not act the way Galen thought they did. The humors were related to four qualities: hot, cold, wet, and dry. Later thinkers who built on Galen's ideas said that each humor had two qualities. Blood was hot and wet, phlegm was cold and wet, yellow bile was hot and dry, and black bile was cold and dry.

Health depended on a balance among the

humors, Galen wrote. If a person had too much or too little of a humor, the balance was disturbed and the person became sick. Many, though not all, earlier doctors had shared this belief. Galen added to it the idea that each part of the body had its own mixture of humors.

Galen also believed that the bodies of different people, even when healthy, had different blends of these liquids. This individual mixture, which he called their constitution or temperament, shaped their appearance and personality.

Each person had one humor that was a little stronger or more plentiful than the others, Galen said. People whose strongest humor was blood were called sanguine [SANG-win]. They had rosy cheeks and a cheerful outlook. People with large amounts of yellow bile, or choler (KOLL-er), were choleric. They were angry most of the time. A lot of black bile made a person melancholic (mel-un-KOLL-ik), or sad. If phlegm was a person's main humor, that person was phlegmatic (fleg MAT ik). Phlegmatic people were calm and hard to upset. People still sometimes use these words to describe different types of personality. Doctors no longer say that humors produce them, however.

Choosing a Treatment

Like Hippocrates, Galen believed that time and Nature were the best healers. Often a person's body could restore its own balance of humors or repair damage done to it. The physician stepped in only when the body was not strong enough to heal itself.

The treatment a physician prescribed, Galen wrote, should depend on several things. The kind of disease was one of these, of course. Others were the part of the body in which the problem appeared, the constitution and strength of the patient, and conditions in the environment that might affect the illness. The stage the sickness had reached was also very important. Galen, like Hippocrates, thought that each disease followed a certain pattern, or course, as it progressed. Recognizing the stages in this pattern was a vital part of both prognosis and treatment.

Like many other physicians of his time, Galen usually treated disease by trying to put the body's humors back into balance. If an illness was thought to have been caused by too much blood, for instance, he would draw blood from the patient to get rid of the extra humor. Drugs

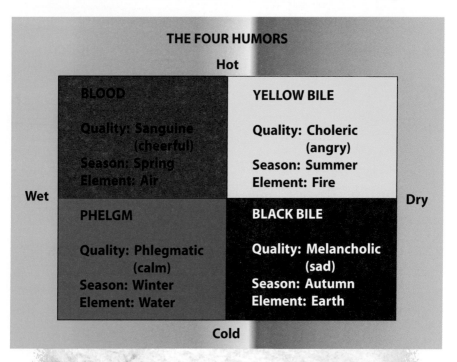

THE FOUR HUMORS

Hot

BLOOD	YELLOW BILE
Quality: Sanguine (cheerful)	Quality: Choleric (angry)
Season: Spring	Season: Summer
Element: Air	Element: Fire
PHELGM	BLACK BILE
Quality: Phlegmatic (calm)	Quality: Melancholic (sad)
Season: Winter	Season: Autumn
Element: Water	Element: Earth

Wet

Dry

Cold

The four humors were associated with different personality traits, seasons, and even the four elements ancient scientists believed made up the physical universe.

that made people vomit or move their bowels were also used to remove excessive humors. Other medicines might add qualities that the patient appeared to lack. Each kind of drug was believed to have its own mixture of qualities.

Selecting Drugs

Galen's version of the humor theory helped him tailor his treatments to individual patients. Unlike some other doctors of his day, he did not believe that people with the same disease should always be given the same drugs. Because people had different balances of humors when they were healthy, he said they might need different combinations of medicines to restore their health.

Galen tried harder than most doctors of his time to find out exactly how and why medicines worked. He learned what effects they had on different parts of the body. This knowledge, too, helped him choose the right drug or drugs for each patient.

Just as he did with pulses, Galen created a

complex system for classifying drugs. He rated them by their strength as well as their qualities. He realized that even a small amount of a strong drug might be dangerous. On the other hand, a weak drug might have no effect unless a large dose of it was given.

Knowing the strength of different drugs was even more important when the drugs were

Galen and other ancient physicians believed an imbalance of the four humors (blood, yellow bile, phelgm, and black bile) caused illnesses. This Greek vase from the fifth century B.C. depicts a surgeon bleeding a patient to restore his health.

combined. "The majority of people cannot even . . . estimate the qualities and defects of any of these ingredients [in a medical mixture] singly," Galen wrote. "Hence also they are ignorant how far they correspond in strength to each other" when mixed.[10] He also said that the action of some drugs changed when different substances were blended with them. When he made mixtures of drugs, perhaps remembering the mathematics he had learned from his father, he carefully weighed every ingredient he put in. He wrote down how much of each material went into the compounds.

One of Galen's most complex mixtures was a drug called theriac. It was supposed to make a person resistant to poison. (It was first used to treat animal bites—therion means "wild animal" in Greek, especially a poisonous animal—then extended to poisons themselves.) Galen gave a daily dose of theriac to Marcus Aurelius, who, like other rulers of his time, feared that people might try to poison him.

Earlier rulers and their doctors had invented

A Roman woman rubs an ointment Galen has mixed for her onto her arm. Galen recorded how to make and administer medicinal compounds in his books.

several kinds of theriac. One form that Galen used had sixty ingredients, including the flesh of poisonous snakes. It also contained juice from the opium poppy, a narcotic. Galen gave Marcus Aurelius this kind of theriac only when the emperor had trouble sleeping. Galen wrote a whole book about theriacs, and physicians continued to use his recipes for more than a thousand years. They prescribed theriacs as a kind of tonic, to help people stay healthy.[11]

Most of the time, Galen made his own drugs. He claimed that he personally picked the plants and gathered the other substances he used. He did not like to buy such things in the marketplace, he said, because the people who sold them often lied about what was in their wares. Whenever he traveled, as he did from time to time throughout his life, he collected samples of healing plants, minerals, and animal products. At home in Rome, he raided the palace storehouses for gifts of rare herbs that had been sent to the emperor. All these things went into his medicines.

In books such as *On the Composition of Drugs,* Galen left descriptions or recipes for making hundreds of different medicines. Most of these were not new, but few other writers had collected so much information about drugs in one place. Galen also corrected or improved many of the drug recipes he learned from others. Some of his remedies were still used in the early twentieth century.[12]

Changing Habits for Health

Drugs were far from the only kind of treatment Galen used. For instance, he often urged changes in what would now be called lifestyle, especially people's choices of food and drink. He wrote several books about diet, in fact. A bad diet could produce illness, he said, and a good one could both restore and maintain health. Modern nutritionists would agree with most of his ideas about food, except perhaps his belief that fresh fruit often caused illness. He recommended taking all foods and drinks in moderate amounts. He encouraged people to exercise, but here, too, he warned against doing too much.

Galen surely must have performed his share of surgery during his years with the gladiators in Pergamum. He probably did a few operations later, too. He seems to have thought of surgery as a last resort, however. This was not surprising, since operations in his day (and, indeed, until the late nineteenth century) had to be performed without anesthesia or any way to prevent infection. This meant that even minor surgery was painful at best and a possible death sentence at worst. Galen wrote that skilled doctors should be able to treat most conditions with drugs rather than operations.

Above all, Galen tried to persuade his patients and friends to live in a way that would keep them from becoming sick in the first place. Like some other ancient thinkers, such as Plato, he believed that preserving health was more the patient's job than the physician's. Galen thought that many diseases were caused by bad habits. Staying healthy, therefore, became a kind of moral duty—the duty to learn which ways of behaving were healthy and then to act in those ways. P. N. Singer, a modern translator of Galen's works, wrote that Galen seemed to think that not only good doctors but also all healthy people should be philosophers. In other words, they should live the kind of quiet life that Galen found to be ideal, as thinking individuals using logic in the pursuit of truth.[13]

5

MEDICINE FOR THE AGES

DURING GALEN'S LIFETIME, COPIES OF his books spread around the Mediterranean world. Unlike some other famous doctors of his day, who tried to hide their "trade secrets," he also claimed to have taught many students. For about one hundred fifty years after his death, though, Galen's ideas—and those of other ancient physicians—seemed to vanish. Historian Vivian Nutton calls this period "a black hole in the history of medicine."[1]

Part of the problem came from changes in society. "Barbarian" tribes, like the ones Marcus Aurelius fought, attacked the Roman Empire in growing numbers. The empire was also governed by bad emperors and torn almost constantly by civil war. Another historian, Owsei Temkin, refers to this time as an "age of anxiety."[2] With so much disturbance around them, few people had the opportunity or desire to gain the kind of education Galen had boasted.

The Byzantine Empire

In 324, the Roman emperor Constantine decided to move his capital to the site of an old Greek city called Byzantium. This city was located on a key spot that links Europe and Asia. Constantine built a new city there and named it New Rome. He made it his official capital in 330. After his death in 337, it was renamed Constantinople. (Today it is Istanbul, Turkey.) It became the center of what later historians called the Byzantine Empire, after the old name for its capital city. This empire grew in strength as the old Roman Empire west of it collapsed.

Moving the capital was not the only major change that Constantine brought. He also turned the empire toward Christianity. In Galen's time, the Christians had been a small religious minority. Roman emperors often persecuted them. After Constantine converted to their religion on his deathbed, however, their power swelled. The emperor Theodosius made Christianity the only legal religion in the empire in 395.

Galen had had mixed feelings about the Christians. On the one hand, he thought them foolish because they believed in miracles. He said that Nature, the only god he recognized, could not break its own rules in this way. At the same time, he admired their quiet, dignified way of life.

The early Christian Church, in turn, was divided in its views of Galen. Many church leaders turned away from science generally. They thought that learning about earthly things, including the human body, was not important. Only the soul or spirit mattered to them. They also rejected ancient writers because those writers had not been Christian.

Galen, however, kept more respect than most. Even though he had not been a Christian, many of his ideas fitted well with the early church's teachings. He believed in a single deity who had created everything in a perfect form. He had urged doctors to care for poor people and not accept payment. Christians shared these values.

Greek literature, including literature about medicine, continued to flourish in the Byzantine Empire. Writers such as Oribasius (325–403), a fellow Pergamene, produced encyclopedias of medicine in Greek that summarized the works of Galen and other famous ancient physicians. These books, which later writers modified and added to, became the medical textbooks of their time. Several of the encyclopedias' authors stated that Galen should be considered the highest authority in medicine.

Lost and Found

By contrast, in the kingdoms that slowly replaced Roman rule in western Europe, the memory of Galen faded. For the most part, his works were read—if at all—only in translation. Unlike the Byzantine Church, the Christian

Church in the West used Latin in all of its official documents, and some monasteries specialized in translating Greek writings into Latin. Some of Galen's books were among those that the monks copied. Books of any kind were rare, however. Doctors usually learned medicine by working with experienced physicians, just as most had done in Galen's own time.

Galen's light burned more brightly in the Middle East. The Nestorians, a Christian sect living in Syria, translated some of his books, along with those of other ancient writers, from Greek into Syraic. These works became part of the inheritance of Muslim culture after the religion of Islam was founded in 622 and Muslim armies seized control of Palestine, Syria, and Egypt in the 630s and 640s. Islam's holy book, the Koran, urged Muslims to learn "foreign sciences," and when Baghdad (now the capital of Iraq) became the chief city of the new Muslim empire, a brilliant group of scholars began to translate works from Greek, Syraic, Sanskrit (the language of Hindu India), Aramaic, and other languages into Arabic. For instance, Hunayn ibn Ishaq (808–873), a court physician in Baghdad who has sometimes been called the "prince of translators," sought out original manuscripts in Greek, including Galen's *On Anatomical Procedures* and *On Medical Experience,* and translated them directly into Arabic. Galen's teachings, in fact, became one of the cornerstones of Islamic medicine. Some well-known Jewish physicians in the Middle East, such as Moses Maimonides (1135–1204), also preserved and admired Galen's medical ideas.

Universities Arise

In the eleventh and twelfth centuries, during the height of the historical period now called the Middle Ages (about 400–1400), society in western Europe changed again. Countries began to unite under strong leaders. Cities, which had shrunk after the fall of the Roman Empire, filled with people once more. The Christian Church was still very powerful, but it was no longer the only center of learning or ideas. Scholars in western Europe began to have more contact with Muslim and Byzantine cultures. These cultures, in turn, helped Europeans rediscover Galen. Galen's writings about the practice of medicine were translated from Arabic or other languages into Latin, which most educated Europeans could read. Older Latin translations were revised.

The first European universities were being founded at this time. Some, such as the universities of Bologna (Italy) and Paris (France), taught medicine as an advanced subject. Salerno, in southwestern Italy, even had a famous school that taught medicine alone. The most highly regarded doctors studied at these universities. The texts they read in their classrooms were sure to carry Galen's name. Indeed, Galen's ideas—or what their teachers said were Galen's ideas—had come to define what medicine was. Most other ancient physicians were forgotten. The few who were remembered, such as Hippocrates, were understood as Galen had described them.

In fact, those medieval doctors never saw Galen's own words. The books they read had been translated—often several times—from his original Greek. Making a translation say exactly the same thing as the original is hard, because every language is different. Some translators, too, had cut out parts of what Galen wrote. Others had added comments and ideas of their own. They did not always tell readers about these changes.

Set in Stone

Worse still, by this time, the many volumes of Galen's writings had been boiled down to just a few sets of rules. They were almost like a second Bible. No one was supposed to question, change, or add to them. Galen's own doubts had been edited out.

In some ways, being seen as a kind of medical god might have pleased Galen. After all, he had written over and over that he knew more than other doctors. He had often claimed that he was finishing the task of developing medicine that

Hippocrates and other early physicians had started. He had tried very hard, too, to tie all his ideas into a single grand system. For the most part, he had succeeded—perhaps too well.

In other ways, though, medieval people's treatment of Galen would have made him angry. It left out a very important part of his teachings: the idea that people should learn about human bodies and medicine through their own experience. He would not have wanted doctors to accept the word of any authority—even himself—without question.

Galen Is Reborn

Galen gained a chance to speak for himself again after 1453. In that year the Turks conquered Constantinople, ending what was left of the Byzantine Empire. Greek scholars from the empire fled to Europe, bringing ancient books with them. Some of those books were Galen's.

Europeans began to learn Greek and make their own translations from that language into

Latin. They felt that they were "purifying" Galen and other ancient writers from the mistakes that had gathered around their work during the past thousand years. Aided by a new invention, the printing press, they published a number of Galen's works in both Latin and the original Greek. The first European edition of Galen's collected works in Greek was published in 1525.

At first, the new editions made Galen's fame and authority greater than ever. During this period, called the Renaissance, however, a new attitude was arising. (*Renaissance* means "rebirth.") People became eager to learn about the world for themselves once more. Some began to question the authority of the church. Others turned their doubting eyes on ancient writers—including Galen.

A New Look at the Body

Starting in the 1300s, dissection of human bodies had become legal again. Medical schools held one or two public dissections a year. As in long-ago Alexandria, the bodies of executed criminals were used. During such dissections, students gathered around and watched as a surgeon cut up the body. An assistant pointed out important features. Meanwhile, a professor read aloud what Galen had said the audience should be seeing.

That was not enough for some onlookers. One of these was a man from Belgium (or Flanders, as people would have said then). He was born Andreas von Wesel in 1514 but called himself Vesalius, the Latinized form of his name. He studied medicine at the university in Paris as a young man. Although Vesalius greatly respected Galen, he sometimes pointed out to his teachers that parts of the body revealed in dissections did not match Galen's descriptions. The professors simply replied that bodies must have changed a little since Galen's day.

Vesalius did not believe them. Forced to leave Paris because of a war between his home country and France, he returned to Belgium and decided to study anatomy on his own. Late one night he stole out to a spot where a criminal had recently

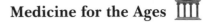

Flemish anatomist and doctor Andreas Vesalius (1514–1564) dared to challenge Galen, who had been the authority on Western medicine for hundreds of years. By dissecting human corpses, Vesalius was able to see where Galen went wrong in his anatomical descriptions and correct some of the mistakes.

been hanged. The body still dangled from its noose, a warning to others who might plan a life of crime. Vesalius cut the body down and took it back to his rooms. There, just as Galen had done with monkeys and other animals almost fourteen hundred years before, he slowly took the body apart and made notes of what he saw. He kept the skeleton for later study.

In addition to these secret experiments, Vesalius studied medicine at the University of Leuven (Belgium). He completed his medical training at the university medical school in Padua, Italy. This school had replaced Salerno as the best-known medical school of its time. The university hired the brilliant young man as a professor of anatomy as soon as he had earned his doctor's degree.

While he was teaching in Padua, Vesalius went on with his anatomy research. He rediscovered the fact that Galen had done all his dissections on animals. Galen had never tried to hide this, but it had been forgotten over the centuries. Vesalius announced that differences between humans and monkeys had led Galen to make many mistakes about human anatomy. "How much has been attributed to Galen . . . by those physicians and anatomists who have followed him, and often against reason!" he wrote later.[3]

After many dissections, Vesalius wrote a book describing what he had learned about anatomy. He hired an artist to make drawings for the book that pictured each system of the body. One picture showed all the bones, for instance. Another showed all of the muscles.

Vesalius called his book *De Humani Corporis Fabrica*. Translated into English, this Latin title means *On the Workings of the Human Body*.

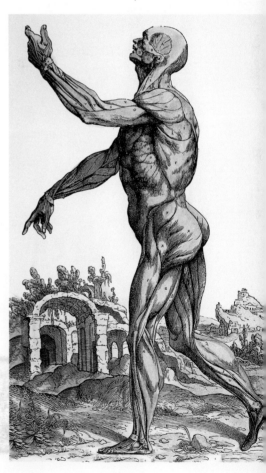

A drawing of the muscles viewed from the side from Vesalius's book.

ANDREAE VESALII
BRVXELLENSIS, SCHOLAE
medicorum Patauinæ profeſſoris, de
Humani corporis fabrica
Libri ſeptem.

CVM CAESAREAE
Maieſt.GalliarumRegis,ac Senatus Veneti gra-
tia & priuilegio, ut in diplomatis eorundem continetur

The title page of Vesalius's book *De Humani Corporis Fabrica* shows Vesalius performing a dissection in an anatomical theater. *De Humani Corporis Fabrica* still serves as the model for modern textbooks on anatomy.

The book was published in 1543—a good year for world-changing writings, it seems. In that same year, Polish astronomer Nicolaus Copernicus published a book proving that the earth went around the sun, not the other way around as had been thought.

Vesalius's book, like Copernicus's, deeply shocked the people of his time. Some physicians and professors, including one of his own former teachers, criticized Vesalius for daring to argue with Galen. Disapproval was so strong, in fact, that Vesalius quit his teaching job and left Padua. Other people, however, hailed his work as revolutionary.

Understanding the Heart

About sixty years after Vesalius published his book, a young Englishman named William Harvey attended the same medical school in Padua that had hired the Belgian. Harvey's professors still repeated Galen's ideas, but Harvey surely heard about Vesalius, too. Perhaps that anatomist's work inspired Harvey to ask his own questions about what Galen had said. Decades afterward, back in England, Harvey proved that some of Galen's physiology was as wrong as his anatomy.

Harvey focused on the heart and blood. As Galen had done, he dissected and experimented only on animals, but he reached different conclusions than Galen had. He showed that the blood was not constantly made and used up as Galen had thought. Instead, it flowed through the body in a circle, over and over. The heart acted like a pump, pushing blood into the arteries. The blood flowed back to the heart through the veins. (Just as Erasistratus and Galen had guessed, arteries and veins are connected by tiny vessels, now called capillaries. These vessels are too small to see without a microscope. An Italian scientist, Marcello Malpighi, discovered them three years after Harvey's death.)

Indeed, Harvey demonstrated, the blood moves in two circles. The larger circle flows through the body. The smaller one goes from the right lower chamber (ventricle) of the heart to the lungs, then back again to the heart's top left chamber (atrium). This circle showed how blood got from one side of the heart to the other, which had puzzled Galen. Harvey proved that the pores that Galen had claimed were in the wall of the heart do not really exist.

Harvey published his conclusions about the heart and circulation in a small book called *De Motu Cordis [On the Motion of the Heart]* in 1628. Like Vesalius's ideas, Harvey's were disbelieved at first.

The English physician William Harvey (1578–1657) disproved Galen's theory that blood is continuously produced and consumed. Harvey demonstrated how blood circulates throughout the body by performing dissections and conducting experiments.

However, Harvey lived to see them accepted by most doctors.

It is hard to know what Galen would have thought about people like Vesalius and Harvey. He never liked to admit that he was wrong, so perhaps their doubting would have made him angry. On the other hand, he might have cheered them on because they were doing—and telling others to do—exactly what Galen himself had said doctors should do. They were learning about the body and how it

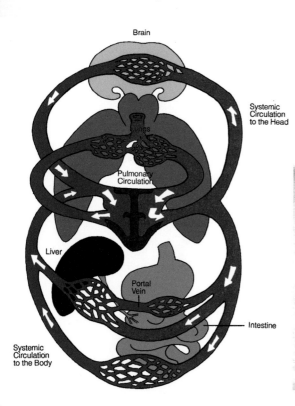

Brain

Systemic Circulation to the Head

Lungs

Pulmonary Circulation

Liver

Portal Vein

Intestine

Systemic Circulation to the Body

Harvey showed that blood moves in circles through the body. One circle goes through the lungs. Red blood vessels carry blood that contains oxygen. Oxygen has been removed from the blood in the blue vessels.

EXERCITATIO
ANATOMICA DE
MOTV CORDIS ET SAN-
GVINIS IN ANIMALI
BVS,
GVILIELMI HARVEI ANGLI,
Medici Regii, & Profeſſoris Anatomiæ in Col-
legio Medicorum Londinenſi.

FRANCOFVRTI,
Sumptibus GVILIELMI FITZERI.
ANNO M. DC. XXVIII.

This is the title page to Harvey's book *De Motu Cordis*.

worked. Even more important, they were observing and experimenting for themselves instead of taking someone else's word. As science historian Benjamin Farrington put it, the work of such men meant that "Galen . . . had triumphed over Galen."[4]

A Pioneer to Remember

Supporters and questioners of Galen fought scientific battles all through the seventeenth century. By the end of the century, the questioners had won. Many of Galen's descriptions of anatomy and physiology, such as his writings about the different kinds of pneuma, were disproved and discarded. Physicians continued to follow some of his advice about medicine, on the other hand, until well into the nineteenth century. For instance, theriac still appeared in several European countries' lists of approved drugs in the late 1800s.

Even though physicians no longer believe most of Galen's ideas, he is worth remembering for several reasons. First, he took anatomy and physiology much further than anyone had before. Some of his findings were wrong, but others, such as his tracing of nerves from the brain and spinal cord, were amazingly accurate. Even more important, he showed doctors that they needed to know how the body was built and how it worked in order to understand and treat disease.

Galen also deserves respect for collecting and preserving so many of the beliefs of ancient medicine. Historians would know much less about early Greek and Roman doctors if Galen had not written about them. He also wove what he saw as the best of those beliefs into a system that was strong and complete enough to support Western medicine almost singlehandedly for fifteen hundred years. Galen's ideas played a large, often dominant, part in medical practice from the mid-fourth century to the mid-nineteenth century—a period that spans about nine tenths of the total history of Western medicine.

Indeed, some of Galen's ideas, and the ideas

he passed on from Hippocrates and others, still underlie what Western physicians think and do. Medical students still dissect human corpses and learn about the body in other ways. Most doctors still see health as a balance among different forces and disease as something that disturbs that balance. Physicians still often ask patients to describe their habits and environment as well as their illness. They still measure patients' pulses and look at their urine. They try to make their treatments fit individual patients as well as their diseases.

Perhaps most important, Galen helped to set up what is now called the scientific method. He said that no scientist should simply accept the word of others, no matter how greatly respected those people were. Instead, researchers should observe for themselves. They should learn about nature by performing experiments and noticing what happens. This advice to "see with your own eyes" is probably Galen's most lasting gift to the world.

ACTIVITIES

Like Galen, you can do experiments to learn about the body and medicine. (Please be sure an adult is present to supervise the first activity.)

Dissecting a Body Part

Materials needed:

❖ a part of a chicken or turkey, such as the leg, breast, or wing
❖ crayons or colored pencils
❖ several sheets of drawing paper
❖ knife

Procedure:

Draw the body part you are working with. Describe what this part does in the living animal. Label any parts of it that you can name, such as skin or the ends of bones. Then, working with an adult, carefully cut the part open to show the structure inside it. Look for such things as bones, muscles, and tendons (the white ropes of tissue that attach muscles to bones). Make one or more drawings of what you find. Label all the things you recognize.

Questions:

What did your dissection tell you about the structure of this body part? What did you learn about the way this body part does its job? How do the different parts within it work together?

Visit to a Doctor

Materials needed:
- ❖ pencil or pen
- ❖ paper for writing

Procedure:

Next time you go to a doctor or take your pet to a veterinarian, make notes of everything that happens. What kinds of questions does the doctor ask? How does he or she examine you or your pet? Does he or she order any tests of blood, urine, or other substances? What treatments does the doctor prescribe?

Questions:

Which of the things your doctor did could Galen also have done for his patients? Do you think Galen would have done them in the same way, or differently? Which ones could Galen not have done? Use library books or the Internet to learn when these newer devices or procedures were invented.

Sports Medicine

Materials needed:

- ❖ newspaper and magazine articles about sports
- ❖ pencil or pen
- ❖ paper for writing

Procedure:

Sports today are not as violent as they were for Galen's gladiators. Players in most sports, however, still risk becoming injured. Different kinds of injuries occur in different kinds of sports. Collect newspaper or magazine stories about players in various sports who become injured. Look, too, for articles about ways sports players keep themselves strong and healthy, such as following a certain diet. Write down what you find out.

Questions:

List several different sports about which you found articles. What kinds of injuries are common in each sport? How did doctors treat those injuries? What do players and their doctors do to prevent such injuries? What do they do to keep up their strength and health?

CHRONOLOGY

A.D. 129—Galen is born in September in Pergamum, Asia Minor.

135–143—Galen's father, Nicon, educates him at home.

143—Galen begins hearing lectures by philosophers.

145—Nicon has a dream in which Asclepius, the god of healing, tells him that Galen should become a physician.

145–149—Galen studies medicine in Pergamum.

149—Nicon dies.

149–152—Galen studies medicine in Smyrna and Corinth.

152–157—Galen studies medicine and anatomy in Alexandria.

157–161—Galen is physician to a troop of gladiators in Pergamum.

161—Marcus Aurelius and Lucius Verus Antoninus become co-emperors of Rome.

162—Galen moves to Rome in the summer; Galen begins seeing patients and cures Eudemus and wife of Boethius.

163–166—Galen gives public demonstrations and

debates medicine with other doctors; Galen
meets wealthy Romans, including the
emperor Marcus Aurelius.

166—Feeling threatened by jealous rivals in Rome,
Galen returns to Pergamum in the summer.

168—Galen is ordered to attend the emperors and
their army in Aquileia toward the end of the
year; Galen treats Marcus Aurelius for a
stomach complaint; Lucius Verus dies during
return trip to Rome, making Marcus
Aurelius sole emperor.

169—Galen returns to Rome early in the year;
Galen becomes physician to Commodus,
Marcus Aurelius's young son and heir.

169–175—Galen lives in country houses with
Commodus's court; Galen does research and
writes many books, including *On the Uses of
Parts*.

175–180—Galen is personal physician to Marcus
Aurelius.

180—Marcus Aurelius dies; Commodus becomes
emperor.

180–192—Galen is personal physician to
Commodus.

192—Commodus is murdered; a fire in the Temple
of Peace destroys some of Galen's
manuscripts.

210 (or later)—Galen dies.

CHAPTER NOTES

Chapter 1. A Dream Career

1. Galen, *On the Affections and Errors of the Soul*, in *Galen: Selected Works*, ed. and trans. P. N. Singer (Oxford, England: Oxford University Press, 1997), p. 119.

2. Galen, *On the Affections and Errors of the Soul*, in *Greek Medicine*, ed. and trans. Arthur J. Brock (New York: AMS Press reprint of 1929 edition, 1977), p. 171.

3. Galen, quoted in *Galen on Examinations by Which the Best Physicians Are Recognized*, ed. and trans. Albert Z. Iskandar (Berlin: Akademie-Verlag, 1988), pp. 101, 103.

4. Ibid., pp. 103, 105.

5. John Scarborough, "Galen and the Gladiators," *Episteme*, vol. 5, no. 2, April–June 1971, pp. 106, 109–110, and Guido Majno, *The Healing Hand: Man and Wound in the Ancient World* (Cambridge, Mass.: Harvard University Press, 1975), pp. 400, 403.

6. Iskandar, p. 105.

Chapter 2. First Among Physicians

1. Vivian Nutton, *Ancient Medicine* (New York: Routledge, 2004), pp. 152–153.

2. P. N. Singer, *Galen: Selected Works* (Oxford, England: Oxford University Press, 1997), xix.

3. Vivian Nutton, trans., *Galen: On Prognosis* (Berlin: Akademie-Verlag, 1979), p. 82.

4. Guido Majno, *The Healing Hand: Man and Wound in the Ancient World* (Cambridge, Mass.: Harvard University Press, 1975), p. 410.

5. Nutton, *Galen: On Prognosis*, p. 119.

6. The introduction to Singer, *Galen: Selected Works*, p. xx, says that this event happened while Marcus Aurelius and Galen were on campaign.

7. Nutton, *Galen: On Prognosis*, p. 129.

8. G. E. R. Lloyd, *Greek Science After Aristotle* (New York: W. W. Norton, 1973), p. 136.

9. Nutton, *Ancient Medicine*, p. 227.

10. Ibid., p. 226.

11. Galen, quoted in *The Greatest Benefit to Mankind: A Medical History of Humanity*, by Roy Porter (New York: Norton, 1997), p. 77.

12. Vivian Nutton, "Logic, Learning, and Experimental Medicine," *Science*, vol. 295, no. 5556, February 1, 2002, p. 800.

Chapter 3. Exploring the Body

1. Galen, *On Anatomical Procedures*, quoted in *Greek Science After Aristotle*, by G. E. R. Lloyd (New York: W. W. Norton, 1973), p. 151.

2. John Scarborough, "Galen's Dissection of the Elephant," *Koroth*, vol. 8, no. 11–12, 1985, p. 125.

3. Galen, *On the Uses of Parts*, quoted in *Doctors: The Biography of Medicine*, by Sherwin B. Nuland (New York: Random House/Vintage, 1989), p. 47.

4. Galen, *On Anatomical Procedures*, in *Greek Medicine*, ed. and trans. Arthur J. Brock (New York: AMS Press reprint of 1929 edition, 1977), p. 160.

5. Ibid., p. 161.

6. Ibid., p. 162.

7. Galen, quoted in Nuland, *Doctors: The Biography of Medicine*, p. 50.

8. Galen, *On the Uses of Parts*, in Brock, *Greek Medicine*, p. 155.

9. Galen, *On the Use of the Pulse*, in *Galen on Respiraton and the Arteries*, ed. and trans. David J. Furley and J. S. Wilkie (Princeton, N.J.: Princeton University Press, 1984), p. 207.

Chapter 4. Healing the Sick

1. Vivian Nutton, trans., *Galen: On Prognosis* (Berlin: Akademie-Verlag, 1979), p. 70.

2. Ibid.

3. Galen, *On the Method of Healing,* quoted in "Galen as a Clinician: His Methods in Diagnosis," by Luis García-Ballester, in *Luis García-Ballester: Galen and Galenism,* by Jon Arrizabalaga et al. (Aldershot, Hampshire, U.K.: Ashgate Variorum, 2002), p. 1654.

4. Galen, quoted in *Ancient Medicine,* by Vivian Nutton (New York: Routledge, 2004), p. 238.

5. Galen, quoted in García-Ballester, p. 1658.

6. Galen, quoted in "Galen (A.D. 129–200) of Pergamun," by P. M. Dunn, *Archives of Disease in Childhood, Fetal and Neonatal Edition,* vol. 88, no. 5, September 2003, p. F441.

7. Nutton, *Ancient Medicine,* p. 236.

8. Galen, *On Affected Parts,* quoted in García-Ballester, p. 1663.

9. P. N. Singer, *Galen: Selected Works* (Oxford, England: Oxford University Press, 1997), x.

10. Galen, *On Antidotes,* in *Greek Medicine,* ed. and trans. Arthur J. Brock (New York: AMS Press reprint of 1929 edition, 1977), p. 198.

11. John Scarborough, "Drugs for an Emperor," *Amphora,* vol. 3, no. 1, Spring 2004, pp. 4–5, 17.

12. Sherwin B. Nuland, *Doctors: The Biography of*

Medicine (New York: Random House/Vintage, 1989), p. 53.

13. Singer, *Galen: Selected Works*, xxxix.

Chapter 5. Medicine for the Ages

1. Vivian Nutton, *Ancient Medicine* (New York: Routledge, 2004), p. 292.

2. Owsei Temkin, *Galenism: Rise and Decline of a Medical Philosophy* (Ithaca: Cornell University Press, 1973), p. 57.

3. Vesalius, quoted in *The Greatest Benefit to Mankind: A Medical History of Humanity*, by Roy Porter (New York: Norton, 1997), p. 181.

4. Benjamin Farrington, *Greek Science: Its Meaning for Us* (New York: Penguin/Pelican, 1949), p. 160.

GLOSSARY

anatomy—The structure of the body.

aorta—The largest artery in the human body. It carries blood out of the left ventricle of the heart.

arteries—Vessels that carry blood away from the heart into the rest of the body.

Asclepius—The Greek god of medicine. He is a son of Apollo, the sun god.

atrium—One of the two upper chambers of the heart in humans.

Barbary ape—Old name for an African monkey now called the macaque. It was Galen's favorite animal to dissect because he thought it was more like humans than any other animal.

black bile—In Galen's medical theory, one of the four humors (fluids) in the body. It does not really exist.

capillaries—Microscopic blood vessels that connect arteries to veins. Erasistratus and Galen said such vessels had to exist, but they were not actually discovered until many hundreds of years later.

choleric—In Galen's medical theory, a term describing a person whose body contained a large amount of the humor called yellow bile (choler). Choleric people were expected to be angry often.

contract—Pull together to become smaller; said of muscles.

course—The pattern of stages that a disease follows over time.

diagnosis—A statement naming the kind of disease a patient has and its cause.

diaphragm—The muscle on the floor of the chest that moves up and down during breathing.

dissect—Cut apart a body for the purpose of learning about its structure.

Dogmatists—Members of a medical sect of Galen's time who believed that theory and logic should be more important to a doctor than observation.

Empiricists—Members of a medical sect of Galen's time who believed that observation was more important to a doctor than theory.

gladiator—In the ancient world, a fighter who took part in sports contests. Many were seriously injured during their battles.

humors—In Galen's medical theory, four fluids in the body (blood, phlegm, yellow bile, black bile) whose mixture determines health and disease and also affects physical appearance and personality. Too much or too little of a particular humor can make a person sick.

inflammation—Redness and swelling of a body part caused by disease.

larynx—The voice box, a boxlike structure in the throat that produces the voice by changing the way air flows in the throat. The vocal cords, strips of tissue in the larynx, vibrate to make sounds.

malaria—A blood disease caused by a microscopic parasite. It produces fevers that rise and fall every few days.

medieval—Related to the Middle Ages, a historical period lasting from about 500 to 1500.

melancholic—In Galen's medical theory, a term describing a person whose body contained a large amount of the humor called black bile. Melancholic people were usually sad.

Methodists—Members of a medical sect of Galen's time who followed a simple theory relating all disease to the condition of tiny openings, or pores, in the body. They claimed that a person could learn enough to become a doctor in just six months.

natural spirit (physical spirit)—In Galen's medical theory, one of three types of pneuma that gives the body life. It is made in the liver and nourishes the body.

parasite—A living thing that takes its food from another living thing.

passion—A strong emotion.

philosopher—A professional thinker or "lover of wisdom."

phlegm—In Galen's medical theory, one of the four fluids (humors) in the body. This word now usually means mucus.

phlegmatic—In Galen's medical theory, a term

describing a person whose body contained a large amount of the humor called phlegm. Phlegmatic people were calm and seldom showed strong emotion.

physician—A medical doctor.

physiology—Study of the functions of different parts of the body and the way the parts carry out those functions.

pneuma—A Greek word meaning "air" or "spirit." Galen believed that the human body contained three kinds of pneuma that gave it life: the natural spirit, the vital spirit, and the psychic spirit.

prognosis—A prediction of the course that a disease will follow in a particular patient, including whether the patient will recover.

psychic spirit—In Galen's medical theory, one of the three types of pneuma that gives the body life. It is made in the brain and carried into the body through the nerves. It gave animals the power to move and sense their environment.

pulmonary artery—The vessel that carries blood from the right ventricle of the heart to the lungs.

pulmonary vein—A vessel that carries blood from the lungs to the left atrium of the heart.

pulse—Movement of the arteries caused by the heartbeat. Changes in the speed (rate) or other qualities of the pulse can show that a person is sick and help a doctor find out what illness the person has.

sanguine—In Galen's medical theory, a term describing a person whose body contained an unusually large amount of blood, one of the four humors. Sanguine people had rosy cheeks and were usually cheerful.

sect—A group of people who share particular beliefs or ideas about a subject such as medicine, religion, or philosophy.

spinal cord—A rope of nerves that descends from the brain and runs inside the stack of bones (vertebrae) that make up the backbone or spinal column. Nerves branch out from the spinal cord and travel to all parts of the body. If the spinal cord is cut or injured, parts of the body may become paralyzed, or unable to move.

stress—A disturbed feeling caused by strong emotion. Galen recognized that stress can imitate or cause illness.

symptom—A sign of illness that a doctor can observe.

temperament (constitution)—In Galen's medical theory, the blend of physical body type and personality produced by an individual's particular blend of the four humors.

tendon—A band of tough tissue that attaches a muscle to a bone.

theriac—A complex blend of substances used as a drug to make a person resistant to poison and to maintain health.

ureters—The tubes carrying urine from the kidneys to the bladder.

valve—An opening in, for instance, a blood vessel that opens in only one direction, allowing fluid to flow in the vessel only in that direction.

veins—Vessels that carry blood from the body toward the heart. Blood in the veins is darker in color than that in the arteries.

vena cava—The largest vein in the body. It carries blood into the right atrium of the heart.

ventricle—One of the two lower chambers of the heart in humans.

vertebra—One of the bones that makes up the backbone. The plural is vertebrae. A hollow channel in the centers of the vertebrae contains the spinal cord.

vital spirit—In Galen's medical theory, one of the three types of pneuma that gives the body life. It is made in the heart and provides heat to the body.

vivisection—The act of dissecting or performing surgery on living animals for the purpose of learning about or experimenting on the body.

wonderful net—Name for a mass of blood vessels found at the base of the brain in cattle and some other animals. Galen thought it also existed in humans, but he was mistaken.

yellow bile—In Galen's medical theory, one of the four fluids (humors) in the body. Bile is a real substance—it helps to digest the fat in food—but it does not act the way Galen said it did.

FURTHER READING

Books

Charman, Andrew. *Life and Times in Ancient Rome.* Boston: Kingfisher, 2007.

Dawson, Ian. *Greek and Roman Medicine.* New York: Enchanted Lion Books, 2005.

Malam, John. *Ancient Rome: Time Travel Guide.* Chicago, Ill.: Raintree, 2007.

Townsend, John. *Pills, Powders, and Potions: A History of Medication.* Chicago, Ill.: Raintree, 2006.

Walker, Richard. *Alive: The Living, Breathing Human Body Book.* New York: DK Publishing, 2007.

Internet Addresses

Galen
http://www.hsl.virginia.edu/historical/artifacts/antiqua/galen.cfm

How the Body Works
http://kidshealth.org/kid/htbw/htbw_main_page.html

Surfing the Human Body
http://library.thinkquest.org/J001614F/

INDEX

Malpighi, Marcello, 104
Marcus Aurelius Antoninus, 33, 34,
	40–42, 44, 83, 84, 114, 115
medical practice/Galen
	Aquileia, 40, 115
	debates, 37–40
	demonstrations, 34–37, 114–115
	disease theory, 21–22, 77–79, 87
	humor theory, 77–81
	lifestyle changes, 29, 72, 86–87
	logic in, 68, 69, 73–75
	patient examination, 22, 71–72,
		75–77
	patient relationships, 69–71
	research, 42, 115
	Rome, 32–34, 44–46, 114, 115
	surgery, 27, 86–87
	treatment, 25–29, 79–81
muscles, 57–58

N
nerves, 19, 36–37, 56–58, 61, 75–77
Nicon, 12–17, 114

O
On Affected Parts (Galen), 68, 73, 76
On Anatomical Procedures (Galen), 51, 53,
	55
On Prognosis (Galen), 68, 73, 74
On the Composition of Drugs (Galen), 85
On the Uses of Parts (Galen), 42, 59–60,
	115
*On the Workings of the Human Body (De
	Humani Corporis Fabrica)* (Vesalius),
	101–103

P
Pergamum
	described, 10–12
	Galen's medical practice, 24–29, 114,
		115
	Galen's medical studies, 114

pharmacology, 27, 33, 76–77, 81–85
philosophy, 15, 48–49, 68–69
physicians, early views of, 30–31
physiology, 59–61, 104
Plato, 16, 61, 87
pneuma, 20, 62–65, 108
pores, 39, 63, 105
pulmonary vein, 63
pulse in medicine, 71–73

R
Renaissance, 97
Rome
	debates, public, 37–40
	demonstrations of medicine, 34–37,
		114–115
	early medicine in, 31
	Emperors of, 40, 114
	Galen's medical practice, 32–34,
		44–46, 114, 115
	languages, official, 31–32

S
Smyrna, 17–18, 114
speech, control of, 36–37
surgery, 27, 86–87

T
Temple of Peace
	debates, public, 37–40
	demonstrations of medicine, 34–37,
		114–115
	fire, 46, 115
theriac, 83–84, 108

V
veins, 20, 58–59, 104
vena cava, 62
Verus Antoninus, Lucius, 33, 40, 41,
	114, 115
Vesalius, Andreas, 98–103
vivisection, 35